Revised Edition

Tiger Woods

By Jeff Savage

AMAZING ATHLETES

Lerner Publications Company • Minneapolis

Lerner Publications Company
A division of Lerner Publishing Group, Inc.
241 First Avenue North
Minneapolis, MN 55401 U.S.A.

Website address: www.lernerbooks.com

Library of Congress Cataloging-in-Publication Data

Savage, Jeff, 1961–
    Tiger Woods / by Jeff Savage. — 2nd rev. ed.
        p. cm. — (Amazing athletes)
    Includes bibliographical references and index.
    ISBN 978–0–7613–4921–1 (lib. bdg. : alk. paper)
    1. Woods, Tiger—Juvenile literature. 2. Racially mixed people—United States—Biography—
Juvenile literature. 3. Golfers—United States—Biography—Juvenile literature. I. Title.
GV964.W66S36 2010
796.352092—dc22 [B]   2008054979

Manufactured in the United States of America
2 3 4 5 6 7 – BP – 15 14 13 12 11 10

TABLE OF CONTENTS

Tiger hits a shot at the Arnold Palmer Invitational in 2009.

RETURN TO THE TOP

Tiger Woods is cool under pressure. He has won more **professional** (pro) golf tournaments at his age than anyone else—ever. As the best golfer in the world, Tiger knows how to stay focused.

But this tournament—the Arnold Palmer Invitational—was different. Tiger had not played professional golf for eight months. Surgery on Tiger's left knee had kept him out of the game. Fans around the world were watching to see if Tiger would be as good as he was before surgery.

The Arnold Palmer Invitational was important for another reason. Tiger wanted to test his knee before playing in the Masters Tournament. The Masters is the first of four important golf events played every year. These events are called **majors**. If Tiger's knee felt good during the Arnold Palmer Invitational in March, he knew he would be ready for the Masters in April.

Arnold Palmer is a golf legend. He has won many major tournaments, including the Masters Tournament in 1958, 1960, 1962, and 1964. Palmer is a member of the World Golf Hall of Fame.

Tiger lines up his putt on the 18th green.

Tiger was behind leader Sean O'Hair by five **strokes**. Only nine holes were left to play. Would Tiger be able to catch O'Hair? Tiger chipped away at the lead. By the time they reached the 18th **green**, the two men were tied. If Tiger could sink a 12-foot **putt**, he would win the tournament.

The people in the **gallery** stared as Tiger's ball rolled toward the hole. When the ball fell in, Tiger jumped into the arms of his **caddy**, Steve Williams. Tiger had won the tournament!

The win proved that Tiger was back and feeling healthy. But the big test would come in April at the Masters Tournament. Would Tiger be up to the challenge?

Tiger *(left)* shakes hands with tournament host Arnold Palmer after Tiger's win.

Tiger's big grin shows how much he enjoyed golfing, even at less than two years old!

CUB WITH A CLUB

Eldrick Woods was born December 30, 1975, to Earl and Kultida Woods. His father called the baby Tiger. This was the nickname of a

Vietnamese army officer and friend. In the 1970s, the original Tiger had saved Earl's life during the Vietnam War.

Young Tiger and his parents lived in Cypress, California. Earl got Tiger a small set of clubs when the boy was not yet two years old. Tiger rarely let go of his putter.

Before long, he was playing at his first golf course. On the first hole, it took him eleven strokes to put the ball in the hole. Soon he began appearing on national television shows to show off his special talent.

In 1977, when Tiger was not yet three, he appeared on *The Mike Douglas Show*. He hit a driver and putted with the famous comedian Bob Hope.

At the age of four, Tiger was taking golf seriously. He practiced driving the ball and putting.

Tiger practiced golf nearly every day. He whacked balls at the **driving range** and practiced on the **putting green**. At the age of six, he got his first **hole in one**.

Sometimes, while Tiger was swinging his club, his father would make noises on purpose. He was trying to help Tiger learn to concentrate on his game.

Other times, Tiger and his father played just

to have fun. They would hit the ball while standing on one foot or try to sink putts with their eyes closed.

When Tiger was eight, he began competing in golf tournaments. He played in his first Junior World Championship. This tournament was for boys who were 10 years old and under. Tiger won!

When Tiger was six, his parents gave him a tape that played soft music with a voice that spoke messages. Some of the messages were "I focus and give it my all" and "I believe in me." Tiger played the tape over and over again while practicing his golf swing.

In 1984, Tiger lines up a putt at his first Junior World Championship.

Tiger's real name is Eldrick. His parents, Earl and Kultida, put the first letter of each of their names on both ends of their son's name. They wanted to show him that they will always be at his side.

Soon he was playing and winning everywhere. At the age of 11, he played in over 30 junior tournaments. He won them all.

Tiger's friends played Little League baseball. Tiger preferred golf. But Tiger was not allowed to play golf until he did his homework. His mother, Kultida, made sure of that. She was originally from Thailand, a country in Asia. Tiger felt very proud of his Asian background.

Earl and Tiger had a special bond. Earl's interest in golf sparked Tiger's.

LAUNCHING A CAREER

Tiger's life was a scramble. He traveled with his father to play in golf tournaments everywhere. Sometimes, his father drove all through the night. Other times, they flew in airplanes. Tiger won a tournament in Colorado. He won another in Florida. He won twice in Texas.

Tiger was a skinny kid, but he had a good swing by the time he was in high school.

When Tiger was 14, he had several coaches, together called Team Tiger. One coach was named Jay Brunza. He helped Tiger focus and relax during a match. As a freshman in high school, Tiger was the best golfer on the school team. He was keeping up with his studies too and earned good grades.

In one tournament, Tiger hit a bad shot. Angry with himself, he smacked his club into his bag. Kultida saw him do it. She didn't approve of bad behavior. She reported his action to the officials and asked that Tiger lose two strokes.

In 1991, Tiger won the U.S. Junior **Amateur** Championship. He was the youngest winner ever. So many trophies filled his bedroom, he could barely get to his bed.

Tiger first played against professional golfers at the 1992 Los Angeles Open.

Tiger played in his first professional tournament at the age of 16. Tiger was still an amateur. He was not a pro yet. This meant that Tiger could not earn **prize money**. But he could still compete against—and learn from—great professional golfers.

The event was the 1992 Los Angeles Open at Riviera Country Club. Tiger stood on the first **tee** and hit his shot down the **fairway**. With that, he had become the youngest person ever to play in an event sponsored by the **Professional Golfers' Association (PGA)**. He shot 72 that day and 75 the next. He **missed the cut** by six strokes.

In 1992, Tiger stood six feet tall, but he weighed just 140 pounds. Being thin as a pencil didn't help his golf game. He didn't have the strength to hit the ball long distances. He tried to gain weight any way he could. He ate two dinners. He ate midnight snacks. He lifted weights to get stronger. Eventually, he began to hit the ball farther.

Even though golf was a huge part of Tiger's life, he relaxed with friends. He especially enjoyed playing video games and Ping-Pong. He developed a love for fast food too.

Tiger holds the trophy for having won his first
U.S. Amateur Championship in 1994.

A RISING STAR

Tiger continued to win tournaments and to
get good grades. He earned a place at Stanford
University in northern California. In his first

year, he was the top college golfer in the country. That year, he played in his first U.S. Amateur Championship. Tiger had to defeat one opponent each day to move on to the next round. He won every match. He trailed his final opponent by six strokes before rallying to win on the final hole. It was the greatest come-from-behind win in the history of the tournament.

Tiger finished high school with good grades. Colleges around the country offered him a free education if he would go to their school. Tiger's first choice was Stanford University in California.

In 1995, Tiger became the youngest player ever to compete in the Masters. He made the cut and finished with a four-day total of five over **par**.

The great golfer Nick Faldo *(seated)* watched as Tiger took a big swing at his first Masters Tournament.

Tiger broke several college records and won the U.S. Amateur title twice more. He was ready to turn pro. On August 28, 1996, newspaper reporters and TV crews gathered to hear Tiger announce that he was joining the PGA Tour. Tiger leaned into a microphone and said two words: "Hello, world."

In 1996, Tiger won his third U.S. Amateur Championship in a row. His coaches and his dad *(second from right)* celebrate the victory. Tiger turned pro soon afterward.

The Nike "swoosh" is on Tiger's hats and shirts.

He signed **endorsement** deals with two companies—Nike and Titleist. Both make sports equipment. He would make commercials to advertise their sporting goods. In return, they would pay him $60 million. Tiger was instantly rich.

Nearly all pro golfers are white. Tiger enjoys a mixture of ethnic backgrounds. From his father, he gets his African American, Native American, and white roots. From his mother comes his Asian background, partly Thai and partly Chinese. Tiger sees himself simply as an American. The endorsement companies saw Tiger's youth and background as a big plus in selling their products.

Kultida is often in the crowd during Tiger's matches.

TIGER TIME

Tiger quickly got better while playing his first three pro tournaments. He finished 60th, then 11th, then 6th. Finally, at the Las Vegas Invitational in Nevada, Tiger won his first pro tournament. He was handed the winner's check of $297,000. Two weeks later in Orlando, he won again.

By 1997, Tiger was roaring. He became the first minority golfer to win the famed Masters Tournament. Fifty million TV viewers watched him calmly sink a five-foot putt. His final score broke the record set by Jack Nicklaus, the great golfer of the 1960s and 1970s. Cheers rang out

Wearing his lucky red shirt, Tiger pumps his fist after winning his very first major and his first Masters in 1997.

as Tiger greeted his parents. Tiger buried his head in his dad's shoulders and wept with joy. Then he hugged his mom and cried some more.

Tiger has used his success to help others. The Tiger Woods Foundation holds golf clinics throughout the country. At the clinics, kids get advice about golf and practice their driving and putting skills. The foundation also runs programs that encourage kids to be healthy and to stay in school.

Tiger has not stopped winning since his first victory in Las Vegas. He has won all four majors—the

Tiger works with kids at one of his foundation's golf clinics.

Masters, the British Open Championship, the PGA Championship, and the U.S. Open—at least twice. Only Jack Nicklaus has won more majors.

Tiger is also making news off the golf course. In 2004 he married Elin Nordegren on the island of Barbados. Three years later, Tiger and Elin welcomed a daughter to their family, Sam Alexis Woods. Son Charlie Axel Woods was born in 2009.

The 2006 British Open Championship was special for Tiger. His father, Earl Woods, died just a few months before the tournament. Tiger won the British Open in his father's memory.

"Sam is very excited to be a big sister," Tiger wrote on his website after the birth of Charlie, "and we feel truly blessed to have such a wonderful family."

Before Tiger came along, many considered Jack Nicklaus to be the greatest golfer that had ever lived. When Tiger was 10 years old, he tacked a piece of paper onto his wall. It was a list of golf records that Nicklaus held. Tiger stared at the list each day. His goal was to break those records someday. That time has come.

Tiger breaks more and more records each year. The way he is going, we may soon be calling Tiger Woods the greatest golfer to ever live.

Tiger walks to his ball during the final round of the 2009 Masters Tournament.

Selected Career Highlights

2008 Won U.S. Open for third time
Won Buick Invitational for fourth time in a row

2007 Won PGA Championship for fourth time
Named PGA Player of the Year for the ninth time

2006 Won British Open and PGA Championship, both for the third time

2005 Won Masters Tournament for fourth time and British Open for
second time

2004 Finished top 10 in 14 of 19 events

2003 Named PGA Player of the Year for the fifth time

2002 Won Masters Tournament for the third time
Won U.S. Open for the second time

2001 Won Masters Tournament for the second time
Was reigning champion of all four majors at the same time
Named PGA Player of the Year for the fourth time

2000 Won U.S. Open, British Open, and PGA Championship
Named Male Athlete of the Year by the Associated Press and
PGA Player of the Year, both for the third time
Named *Sports Illustrated* Sportsman of the Year and received
ESPY award as Outstanding Male Athlete of the Year, both
for the second time

1999 Won PGA Championship
Again named Male Athlete of the Year by Associated
Press and PGA Player of the Year

1998 Received ESPY award as Outstanding Male Athlete of
the Year

1997 Won Masters Tournament for the first time

1996 Won first PGA Tour event, Las Vegas Invitational
Named *Sports Illustrated* Sportsman of the Year

1994–1996 While at Stanford University, won U.S.
Amateur Championship three years
in a row

1991–1993 Won U.S. Junior Amateur
Tournament three years in a row

GLOSSARY

amateur: an athlete who receives no prize money for playing in an event

caddy: a person on a golf course who carries the clubs and advises the golfer

driving range: an area where golfers practice hitting golf balls

endorsement: approval of a product in public to help sell it

fairway: on a golf course, the long, grassy area that stretches from the tee (where the ball is first struck) to the green (where the hole is)

gallery: the crowd at a golf tournament

green: on a golf course, the small, grassy area where the hole (cup) is

hole in one: when the ball is hit off the tee and lands in the hole using only one stroke

majors: four international golf tournaments held each year. The tournaments are the Masters, the U.S. Open, the British Open, and the PGA Championship.

miss the cut: to be taken out of competition in a tournament because of having a score that is too high. The score, or cut, is set after players play two (of four) rounds of golf. Players must "make the cut" to get to play the final two rounds.

par: the number of strokes from tee to green a player is supposed to need to get the ball in the hole. One stroke less than par is called a birdie. One stroke more is called a bogey.

prize money: the money awarded to each player, based on his or her finishing score

professional: a player who receives money for playing in an event

Professional Golfers' Association (PGA): the group that oversees the tournaments in which male professional golfers play

putt: to tap the ball gently so it will go in the hole on the green

putting green: a grassy area where golfers practice putting

strokes: hitting golf balls with a club. Also called shots

tee: the area where golfers hit their first shot of each hole. *Tee* is also the name for the wooden peg that a ball is set on.

FURTHER READING & WEBSITES

Glaser, Jason. *Tiger Woods*. New York: PowerKids Press, 2008.

Hasday, Judy L. *Tiger Woods: Athlete*. New York: Chelsea House, 2008.

Parks, Peter. *How to Improve at Golf*. New York: Crabtree Publishing, 2008.

Webster, Christine. *Masters Golf Tournament*. New York: Weigl Publishers, 2009.

PGA Tour
http://www.pgatour.com
A website developed by the Professional Golfers' Association that provides fans with recent news stories, biographies of golfers, and information about tournaments

Sports Illustrated Kids
http://www.sikids.com
The *Sports Illustrated Kids* website that covers all sports, including golf

Tiger's Website
http://www.tigerwoods.com
Tiger's official website, featuring trivia, photos, and information about golf

The Tiger Woods Foundation
http://www.twfound.org
The official website of Tiger's foundation, which runs junior golf clinics and educational programs around the country

INDEX

PHOTO ACKNOWLEDGMENTS

The images in this book are used with the permission of: © David Cannon/ Getty Images, p. 4; © Romeo Guzman/Cal Sport Media/ZUMA Press, p. 6; © David Cannon/Getty Images, p. 7, 20; © David Strick/Redux, p. 8, 10; San Diego Union-Tribune/Dave Siccardi, p. 11; © Ken Levine/Getty Images, p. 12; © Duomo/CORBIS, p. 13, 14; © Gary Newkirk/Allsport/Getty Images, p. 16; © Rusty Jarrett/Allsport/Getty Images, p. 18; © J.D. Cuban/Allsport/ Getty Images, p. 21; © Jamie Squire/Allsport/Getty Images, p. 22; © Craig Jones/Allsport/Getty Images, p. 23, 29; © Stephen Munday/Allsport/Getty Images, p. 25; © Reuters/CORBIS, p. 26; © Don Emmert/AFP/Getty Images, p. 28.

Front Cover: © Mark Ralston/AFP/Getty Images.